50 Cookie and Treat Recipes for Home

By: Kelly Johnson

Table of Contents

- Chocolate Chip Cookies
- Sugar Cookies
- Peanut Butter Cookies
- Oatmeal Raisin Cookies
- Snickerdoodles
- Shortbread Cookies
- Double Chocolate Cookies
- White Chocolate Macadamia Nut Cookies
- Gingerbread Cookies
- Lemon Cookies
- Coconut Macaroons
- M&M Cookies
- Molasses Cookies
- Almond Biscotti
- Thumbprint Cookies
- Butter Cookies
- Linzer Cookies
- Chocolate Crinkle Cookies
- Pecan Sandies
- Biscotti
- Spritz Cookies
- Red Velvet Cookies
- Pumpkin Cookies
- Toffee Cookies
- Raspberry Bars
- Lemon Bars
- Brownies
- Blondies
- Magic Cookie Bars
- Rice Krispie Treats
- Fudge
- Peanut Butter Bars
- S'mores Bars
- Caramel Corn
- Chocolate Bark

- Whoopie Pies
- Macarons
- Madeleines
- Biscotti
- Rocky Road
- Marshmallow Treats
- Truffles
- Chocolate-Covered Pretzels
- Caramel Apples
- Peanut Brittle
- Nougat
- Pecan Pralines
- Chocolate-Covered Cherries
- Fruitcake Cookies
- Black and White Cookies

Chocolate Chip Cookies

Ingredients:

- 2 1/4 cups all-purpose flour
- 1/2 teaspoon baking soda
- 1 cup unsalted butter, room temperature
- 1/2 cup granulated sugar
- 1 cup packed light-brown sugar
- 1 teaspoon salt
- 2 teaspoons pure vanilla extract
- 2 large eggs
- 2 cups semisweet and/or milk chocolate chips

Instructions:

1. Preheat oven to 350°F (175°C). Line baking sheets with parchment paper.
2. In a small bowl, whisk together flour and baking soda; set aside.
3. In the bowl of an electric mixer fitted with the paddle attachment, combine butter with both sugars; beat on medium speed until light and fluffy. Reduce speed to low; add salt, vanilla, and eggs. Beat until well mixed, about 1 minute.
4. Add flour mixture; mix until just combined. Stir in chocolate chips.
5. Drop dough by rounded tablespoons onto prepared baking sheets, spacing about 2 inches apart.
6. Bake until cookies are golden around the edges but still soft in the center, 8 to 10 minutes. Remove from oven, and let cool on baking sheet 1 to 2 minutes. Transfer to a wire rack, and let cool completely.

Sugar Cookies

Ingredients:

- 2 3/4 cups all-purpose flour
- 1 teaspoon baking soda
- 1/2 teaspoon baking powder
- 1 cup unsalted butter, softened
- 1 1/2 cups granulated sugar
- 1 egg
- 1 teaspoon vanilla extract
- 1/2 teaspoon almond extract (optional)
- 3 to 4 tablespoons buttermilk

Instructions:

1. Preheat oven to 375°F (190°C). Line baking sheets with parchment paper.
2. In a small bowl, stir together flour, baking soda, and baking powder. Set aside.
3. In a large bowl, cream together the butter and sugar until smooth. Beat in the egg, vanilla extract, and almond extract (if using).
4. Gradually blend in the dry ingredients. Add buttermilk, 1 tablespoon at a time, until the dough is moist and forms a ball.
5. Roll out dough on a lightly floured surface to 1/4 inch thickness. Cut into shapes with cookie cutters. Place cookies 1 inch apart on prepared baking sheets.
6. Bake 8 to 10 minutes in the preheated oven, or until golden. Let cool on baking sheet for 2 minutes before transferring to wire racks to cool completely.

Peanut Butter Cookies

Ingredients:

- 1 cup unsalted butter, softened
- 1 cup granulated sugar
- 1 cup packed brown sugar
- 1 cup creamy peanut butter
- 2 large eggs
- 2 1/2 cups all-purpose flour
- 1 1/2 teaspoons baking soda
- 1 teaspoon baking powder
- 1/2 teaspoon salt

Instructions:

1. Preheat oven to 350°F (175°C). Line baking sheets with parchment paper.
2. In a large bowl, cream together the butter, granulated sugar, brown sugar, and peanut butter until smooth.
3. Beat in the eggs, one at a time, until well blended.
4. In a separate bowl, whisk together the flour, baking soda, baking powder, and salt. Gradually add to the peanut butter mixture, mixing just until combined.
5. Roll dough into 1-inch balls and place 2 inches apart on the prepared baking sheets. Flatten each ball with a fork, making a crisscross pattern.
6. Bake for 10 to 12 minutes, or until edges are golden. Let cool on baking sheets for a few minutes before transferring to wire racks to cool completely.

Oatmeal Raisin Cookies

Ingredients:

- 1 cup unsalted butter, softened
- 1 cup granulated sugar
- 1 cup packed brown sugar
- 2 large eggs
- 1 teaspoon vanilla extract
- 1 1/2 cups all-purpose flour
- 1 teaspoon baking soda
- 1 teaspoon ground cinnamon
- 1/2 teaspoon salt
- 3 cups old-fashioned rolled oats
- 1 cup raisins

Instructions:

1. Preheat oven to 350°F (175°C). Line baking sheets with parchment paper.
2. In a large bowl, cream together the butter, granulated sugar, and brown sugar until smooth.
3. Beat in the eggs, one at a time, then stir in the vanilla extract.
4. In a separate bowl, whisk together the flour, baking soda, cinnamon, and salt. Gradually add to the butter mixture and mix until just combined.
5. Stir in the oats and raisins.
6. Drop dough by rounded tablespoons onto the prepared baking sheets, spacing about 2 inches apart.
7. Bake for 10 to 12 minutes, or until edges are golden brown. Let cool on baking sheets for a few minutes before transferring to wire racks to cool completely.

Snickerdoodles

Ingredients:

- 2 3/4 cups all-purpose flour
- 1 1/2 teaspoons cream of tartar
- 1 teaspoon baking soda
- 1/2 teaspoon salt
- 1 cup unsalted butter, softened
- 1 1/2 cups granulated sugar
- 2 large eggs
- 1 teaspoon vanilla extract
- 3 tablespoons granulated sugar
- 1 tablespoon ground cinnamon

Instructions:

1. Preheat oven to 375°F (190°C). Line baking sheets with parchment paper.
2. In a medium bowl, whisk together flour, cream of tartar, baking soda, and salt. Set aside.
3. In a large bowl, cream together the butter and 1 1/2 cups granulated sugar until light and fluffy.
4. Beat in the eggs, one at a time, then stir in the vanilla extract.
5. Gradually add the dry ingredients to the butter mixture, mixing until just combined.
6. In a small bowl, mix the remaining 3 tablespoons of granulated sugar with the cinnamon.
7. Roll the dough into 1-inch balls, then roll each ball in the cinnamon-sugar mixture to coat.
8. Place the coated dough balls 2 inches apart on the prepared baking sheets.
9. Bake for 8 to 10 minutes, or until the edges are set and the centers are still soft.
10. Let cool on baking sheets for a few minutes before transferring to wire racks to cool completely.

Shortbread Cookies

Ingredients:

- 1 cup unsalted butter, softened
- 1/2 cup granulated sugar
- 2 cups all-purpose flour
- 1/4 teaspoon salt

Instructions:

1. Preheat oven to 350°F (175°C). Line baking sheets with parchment paper.
2. In a large bowl, cream together the butter and sugar until light and fluffy.
3. Gradually add the flour and salt, mixing until a dough forms.
4. Roll out the dough on a lightly floured surface to about 1/4 inch thickness.
5. Use cookie cutters to cut out desired shapes or simply slice the dough into rectangles or squares.
6. Place the cookies on the prepared baking sheets, spacing them about 1 inch apart.
7. Prick the tops of the cookies with a fork.
8. Bake for 12 to 15 minutes, or until the edges are lightly golden.
9. Let cool on baking sheets for a few minutes before transferring to wire racks to cool completely.

Double Chocolate Cookies

Ingredients:

- 1 cup unsalted butter, softened
- 1 cup granulated sugar
- 3/4 cup packed brown sugar
- 2 large eggs
- 1 teaspoon vanilla extract
- 2 cups all-purpose flour
- 1/2 cup unsweetened cocoa powder
- 1 teaspoon baking soda
- 1/4 teaspoon salt
- 2 cups semisweet chocolate chips

Instructions:

1. Preheat oven to 350°F (175°C). Line baking sheets with parchment paper.
2. In a large bowl, cream together the butter, granulated sugar, and brown sugar until smooth.
3. Beat in the eggs, one at a time, then stir in the vanilla extract.
4. In a separate bowl, whisk together the flour, cocoa powder, baking soda, and salt.
5. Gradually add the dry ingredients to the butter mixture and mix until well combined.
6. Stir in the chocolate chips.
7. Drop dough by rounded tablespoons onto the prepared baking sheets, spacing about 2 inches apart.
8. Bake for 8 to 10 minutes, or until the edges are set and the tops are slightly cracked.
9. Let cool on baking sheets for a few minutes before transferring to wire racks to cool completely.

White Chocolate Macadamia Nut Cookies

Ingredients:

- 1 cup unsalted butter, softened
- 1 cup granulated sugar
- 3/4 cup packed brown sugar
- 2 large eggs
- 1 teaspoon vanilla extract
- 2 1/4 cups all-purpose flour
- 1 teaspoon baking soda
- 1/2 teaspoon salt
- 1 cup white chocolate chips
- 1 cup chopped macadamia nuts

Instructions:

1. Preheat oven to 350°F (175°C). Line baking sheets with parchment paper.
2. In a large bowl, cream together the butter, granulated sugar, and brown sugar until smooth.
3. Beat in the eggs, one at a time, then stir in the vanilla extract.
4. In a separate bowl, whisk together the flour, baking soda, and salt.
5. Gradually add the dry ingredients to the butter mixture and mix until well combined.
6. Stir in the white chocolate chips and chopped macadamia nuts.
7. Drop dough by rounded tablespoons onto the prepared baking sheets, spacing about 2 inches apart.
8. Bake for 10 to 12 minutes, or until the edges are golden brown.
9. Let cool on baking sheets for a few minutes before transferring to wire racks to cool completely.

Gingerbread Cookies

Ingredients:

- 3 cups all-purpose flour
- 1 teaspoon baking soda
- 1/4 teaspoon salt
- 1 tablespoon ground ginger
- 1 1/2 teaspoons ground cinnamon
- 1/2 teaspoon ground cloves
- 1/2 cup unsalted butter, softened
- 1/2 cup packed brown sugar
- 1 large egg
- 2/3 cup molasses
- 1 teaspoon vanilla extract

Instructions:

1. In a medium bowl, whisk together the flour, baking soda, salt, ginger, cinnamon, and cloves. Set aside.
2. In a large bowl, cream together the butter and brown sugar until light and fluffy.
3. Beat in the egg, molasses, and vanilla extract until well combined.
4. Gradually add the dry ingredients to the wet ingredients, mixing until a dough forms.
5. Divide the dough in half, wrap each portion in plastic wrap, and refrigerate for at least 1 hour or until firm.
6. Preheat oven to 350°F (175°C). Line baking sheets with parchment paper.
7. On a lightly floured surface, roll out one portion of the dough to about 1/4 inch thickness.
8. Use cookie cutters to cut out desired shapes and place them on the prepared baking sheets, spacing about 1 inch apart.
9. Bake for 8 to 10 minutes, or until edges are set.
10. Let cool on baking sheets for a few minutes before transferring to wire racks to cool completely.
11. Decorate with icing or enjoy as is!

Lemon Cookies

Ingredients:

- 2 1/4 cups all-purpose flour
- 1/2 teaspoon baking powder
- 1/4 teaspoon salt
- 1 cup unsalted butter, softened
- 1 cup granulated sugar
- 2 large eggs
- Zest of 2 lemons
- 2 tablespoons fresh lemon juice
- 1 teaspoon vanilla extract
- Optional: additional granulated sugar for rolling (about 1/4 cup)

Instructions:

1. In a medium bowl, whisk together the flour, baking powder, and salt. Set aside.
2. In a large bowl, cream together the butter and granulated sugar until light and fluffy.
3. Beat in the eggs, one at a time, until well combined.
4. Mix in the lemon zest, lemon juice, and vanilla extract.
5. Gradually add the dry ingredients to the wet ingredients, mixing until a dough forms.
6. Cover the dough and refrigerate for at least 1 hour or until firm.
7. Preheat oven to 350°F (175°C). Line baking sheets with parchment paper.
8. If desired, roll tablespoon-sized portions of dough into balls and then roll them in granulated sugar to coat.
9. Place the coated dough balls on the prepared baking sheets, spacing about 2 inches apart.
10. Flatten each dough ball slightly with the bottom of a glass or your fingers.
11. Bake for 10 to 12 minutes, or until the edges are lightly golden.
12. Let cool on baking sheets for a few minutes before transferring to wire racks to cool completely.

Coconut Macaroons

Ingredients:

- 3 cups shredded coconut (sweetened or unsweetened)
- 3/4 cup sweetened condensed milk
- 2 large egg whites
- 1 teaspoon vanilla extract
- 1/4 teaspoon salt

Instructions:

1. Preheat oven to 325°F (160°C). Line baking sheets with parchment paper.
2. In a large bowl, combine the shredded coconut, sweetened condensed milk, vanilla extract, and salt. Mix well.
3. In a separate bowl, beat the egg whites until stiff peaks form.
4. Gently fold the beaten egg whites into the coconut mixture until fully combined.
5. Drop spoonfuls of the mixture onto the prepared baking sheets, leaving some space between each macaroon.
6. Bake for 20 to 25 minutes, or until the edges are golden brown.
7. Let the macaroons cool on the baking sheets for a few minutes before transferring them to a wire rack to cool completely.
8. Optionally, you can drizzle melted chocolate over the cooled macaroons for extra flavor and decoration. Allow the chocolate to set before serving.

M&M Cookies

Ingredients:

- 2 1/4 cups all-purpose flour
- 1 teaspoon baking soda
- 1/2 teaspoon salt
- 1 cup unsalted butter, softened
- 3/4 cup granulated sugar
- 3/4 cup packed brown sugar
- 1 teaspoon vanilla extract
- 2 large eggs
- 1 1/2 cups M&M's candies

Instructions:

1. Preheat oven to 350°F (175°C). Line baking sheets with parchment paper.
2. In a medium bowl, whisk together the flour, baking soda, and salt. Set aside.
3. In a large bowl, cream together the softened butter, granulated sugar, brown sugar, and vanilla extract until light and fluffy.
4. Beat in the eggs one at a time until well combined.
5. Gradually add the dry ingredients to the wet ingredients, mixing until just combined.
6. Stir in the M&M's candies until evenly distributed throughout the dough.
7. Drop tablespoon-sized portions of dough onto the prepared baking sheets, spacing them about 2 inches apart.
8. Gently press a few extra M&M's candies onto the tops of each cookie dough ball for added decoration, if desired.
9. Bake for 10-12 minutes, or until the edges are lightly golden.
10. Let the cookies cool on the baking sheets for a few minutes before transferring them to wire racks to cool completely. Enjoy!

Molasses Cookies

Ingredients:

- 2 1/4 cups all-purpose flour
- 2 teaspoons baking soda
- 1 teaspoon ground cinnamon
- 1 teaspoon ground ginger
- 1/2 teaspoon ground cloves
- 1/4 teaspoon salt
- 3/4 cup unsalted butter, softened
- 1 cup granulated sugar, plus extra for rolling
- 1 large egg
- 1/4 cup molasses

Instructions:

1. Preheat oven to 375°F (190°C). Line baking sheets with parchment paper.
2. In a medium bowl, whisk together the flour, baking soda, cinnamon, ginger, cloves, and salt. Set aside.
3. In a large bowl, cream together the softened butter and 1 cup granulated sugar until light and fluffy.
4. Beat in the egg until well combined, then stir in the molasses.
5. Gradually add the dry ingredients to the wet ingredients, mixing until just combined.
6. Place some granulated sugar in a shallow bowl for rolling the cookie dough.
7. Roll tablespoon-sized portions of dough into balls, then roll each ball in the granulated sugar until coated.
8. Place the coated dough balls on the prepared baking sheets, spacing them about 2 inches apart.
9. Bake for 8-10 minutes, or until the cookies are set and slightly cracked on top.
10. Let the cookies cool on the baking sheets for a few minutes before transferring them to wire racks to cool completely. Enjoy the rich flavor of molasses in every bite!

Almond Biscotti

Ingredients:

- 2 cups all-purpose flour
- 1 1/2 teaspoons baking powder
- 1/4 teaspoon salt
- 3/4 cup granulated sugar
- 1/2 cup unsalted butter, softened
- 2 large eggs
- 1 teaspoon vanilla extract
- 1 teaspoon almond extract
- 1 cup almonds, chopped

Instructions:

1. Preheat oven to 350°F (175°C). Line a baking sheet with parchment paper.
2. In a medium bowl, whisk together the flour, baking powder, and salt. Set aside.
3. In a large bowl, cream together the softened butter and granulated sugar until light and fluffy.
4. Beat in the eggs, one at a time, until well combined. Stir in the vanilla extract and almond extract.
5. Gradually add the dry ingredients to the wet ingredients, mixing until a dough forms.
6. Fold in the chopped almonds until evenly distributed throughout the dough.
7. Divide the dough in half. On a lightly floured surface, shape each half into a log about 12 inches long and 2 inches wide.
8. Place the logs on the prepared baking sheet, spacing them apart. Flatten the tops slightly.
9. Bake for 25-30 minutes, or until the logs are firm to the touch and lightly golden brown.
10. Remove the logs from the oven and let them cool on the baking sheet for 10 minutes. Reduce the oven temperature to 325°F (160°C).
11. Transfer the logs to a cutting board and use a serrated knife to slice them diagonally into 1/2-inch thick slices.
12. Place the slices back on the baking sheet, cut side down. Bake for an additional 10-15 minutes, or until the biscotti are crisp and golden brown.
13. Let the biscotti cool completely on wire racks before serving. Enjoy with a cup of coffee or tea!

Thumbprint Cookies

Ingredients:

- 1 cup unsalted butter, softened
- 2/3 cup granulated sugar
- 1/2 teaspoon vanilla extract
- 2 cups all-purpose flour
- 1/4 teaspoon salt
- 1 cup finely chopped nuts (such as walnuts or almonds)
- Jam or preserves of your choice

Instructions:

1. Preheat oven to 350°F (175°C). Line baking sheets with parchment paper.
2. In a large bowl, cream together the softened butter, granulated sugar, and vanilla extract until light and fluffy.
3. Gradually add the flour and salt to the creamed mixture, mixing until a dough forms.
4. Shape the dough into 1-inch balls. Roll each ball in the finely chopped nuts until coated.
5. Place the coated dough balls on the prepared baking sheets, spacing them about 1 inch apart.
6. Use your thumb or the back of a teaspoon to make an indentation in the center of each cookie.
7. Fill each indentation with a small amount of jam or preserves.
8. Bake for 10-12 minutes, or until the cookies are set and the edges are lightly golden.
9. Let the cookies cool on the baking sheets for a few minutes before transferring them to wire racks to cool completely.
10. Enjoy these delicious thumbprint cookies with your favorite jam filling!

Butter Cookies

Ingredients:

- 1 cup unsalted butter, softened
- 1 cup granulated sugar
- 1 large egg
- 1 teaspoon vanilla extract
- 2 1/2 cups all-purpose flour
- 1/2 teaspoon baking powder
- 1/4 teaspoon salt

Instructions:

1. Preheat oven to 350°F (175°C). Line baking sheets with parchment paper.
2. In a large bowl, cream together the softened butter and granulated sugar until light and fluffy.
3. Beat in the egg and vanilla extract until well combined.
4. In a separate bowl, whisk together the flour, baking powder, and salt.
5. Gradually add the dry ingredients to the wet ingredients, mixing until a dough forms.
6. Roll out the dough on a lightly floured surface to about 1/4 inch thickness.
7. Use cookie cutters to cut out desired shapes and place them on the prepared baking sheets, spacing them about 1 inch apart.
8. Bake for 8-10 minutes, or until the edges are lightly golden.
9. Let the cookies cool on the baking sheets for a few minutes before transferring them to wire racks to cool completely.
10. Enjoy these classic butter cookies plain or decorate them with icing or sprinkles if desired!

Linzer Cookies

Ingredients:

- 1 cup unsalted butter, softened
- 2/3 cup granulated sugar
- 1 large egg
- 1 teaspoon vanilla extract
- 2 cups all-purpose flour
- 1 cup ground almonds or hazelnuts
- 1/2 teaspoon ground cinnamon
- 1/2 cup raspberry or strawberry jam
- Confectioners' sugar, for dusting

Instructions:

1. In a large bowl, cream together the softened butter and granulated sugar until light and fluffy.
2. Beat in the egg and vanilla extract until well combined.
3. In a separate bowl, whisk together the flour, ground almonds or hazelnuts, and ground cinnamon.
4. Gradually add the dry ingredients to the wet ingredients, mixing until a dough forms.
5. Divide the dough in half. Shape each half into a disk, wrap in plastic wrap, and refrigerate for at least 1 hour or until firm.
6. Preheat oven to 350°F (175°C). Line baking sheets with parchment paper.
7. On a lightly floured surface, roll out one disk of dough to about 1/8 inch thickness.
8. Use a round cookie cutter to cut out circles. Use a smaller cookie cutter to cut out centers from half of the circles, creating a ring shape.
9. Place the solid circles on the prepared baking sheets. Place the ring-shaped cookies on separate baking sheets.
10. Bake for 8-10 minutes, or until the edges are lightly golden. Let cool on baking sheets for a few minutes before transferring to wire racks to cool completely.
11. Once cooled, spread a thin layer of jam onto the solid circles. Top each with a ring-shaped cookie to create sandwiches.
12. Dust the tops of the cookies with confectioners' sugar before serving. Enjoy these delightful Linzer cookies with a cup of tea or coffee!

Chocolate Crinkle Cookies

Ingredients:

- 1 cup unsweetened cocoa powder
- 2 cups granulated sugar
- 1/2 cup vegetable oil
- 4 large eggs
- 2 teaspoons vanilla extract
- 2 cups all-purpose flour
- 2 teaspoons baking powder
- 1/2 teaspoon salt
- 1 cup confectioners' sugar, for coating

Instructions:

1. In a large bowl, whisk together the cocoa powder, granulated sugar, and vegetable oil until well combined.
2. Beat in the eggs, one at a time, until smooth. Stir in the vanilla extract.
3. In a separate bowl, whisk together the flour, baking powder, and salt.
4. Gradually add the dry ingredients to the wet ingredients, mixing until a dough forms. Cover the bowl and refrigerate the dough for at least 4 hours or overnight.
5. Preheat oven to 350°F (175°C). Line baking sheets with parchment paper.
6. Place the confectioners' sugar in a shallow bowl.
7. Use a spoon or cookie scoop to scoop out portions of dough. Roll each portion into a ball, then roll it in the confectioners' sugar until fully coated.
8. Place the coated dough balls on the prepared baking sheets, spacing them about 2 inches apart.
9. Bake for 10-12 minutes, or until the cookies are set and cracked on top.
10. Let the cookies cool on the baking sheets for a few minutes before transferring them to wire racks to cool completely.
11. Enjoy these deliciously chocolatey crinkle cookies with a glass of cold milk or your favorite hot beverage!

Pecan Sandies

Ingredients:

- 1 cup unsalted butter, softened
- 1/2 cup granulated sugar
- 2 teaspoons vanilla extract
- 2 cups all-purpose flour
- 1/4 teaspoon salt
- 1 cup finely chopped pecans
- Additional granulated sugar for rolling (optional)

Instructions:

1. Preheat oven to 350°F (175°C). Line baking sheets with parchment paper.
2. In a large bowl, cream together the softened butter, granulated sugar, and vanilla extract until light and fluffy.
3. In a separate bowl, whisk together the flour and salt.
4. Gradually add the dry ingredients to the creamed mixture, mixing until a dough forms.
5. Stir in the chopped pecans until evenly distributed throughout the dough.
6. If desired, roll tablespoon-sized portions of dough into balls, then roll them in granulated sugar until coated.
7. Place the dough balls on the prepared baking sheets, spacing them about 2 inches apart.
8. Flatten each dough ball slightly with the bottom of a glass or your fingers.
9. Bake for 12-15 minutes, or until the edges are lightly golden.
10. Let the cookies cool on the baking sheets for a few minutes before transferring them to wire racks to cool completely.
11. Enjoy these delicious pecan sandies with a cup of coffee or tea!

Biscotti

Ingredients:

- 2 cups all-purpose flour
- 1 teaspoon baking powder
- 1/4 teaspoon salt
- 3/4 cup granulated sugar
- 1/2 cup unsalted butter, softened
- 2 large eggs
- 1 teaspoon vanilla extract
- 1/2 cup chopped nuts or dried fruits (optional)

Instructions:

1. Preheat oven to 350°F (175°C). Line a baking sheet with parchment paper.
2. In a medium bowl, whisk together the flour, baking powder, and salt. Set aside.
3. In a large bowl, cream together the softened butter and granulated sugar until light and fluffy.
4. Beat in the eggs, one at a time, until well combined. Stir in the vanilla extract.
5. Gradually add the dry ingredients to the wet ingredients, mixing until a dough forms. If using nuts or dried fruits, fold them into the dough until evenly distributed.
6. Divide the dough in half. On the prepared baking sheet, shape each half into a log about 12 inches long and 2 inches wide.
7. Bake for 25-30 minutes, or until the logs are firm to the touch and lightly golden brown.
8. Remove the baking sheet from the oven and let the logs cool for 10 minutes. Reduce the oven temperature to 325°F (160°C).
9. Transfer the logs to a cutting board and use a serrated knife to slice them diagonally into 1/2-inch thick slices.
10. Place the slices back on the baking sheet, cut side down. Bake for an additional 10-15 minutes, or until the biscotti are crisp and lightly golden brown.
11. Let the biscotti cool completely on wire racks before serving. Enjoy these crunchy Italian cookies with a cup of coffee or tea!

Spritz Cookies

Ingredients:

- 1 cup unsalted butter, softened
- 2/3 cup granulated sugar
- 1 large egg
- 1 teaspoon vanilla extract
- 1/4 teaspoon almond extract (optional)
- 2 1/4 cups all-purpose flour
- 1/2 teaspoon baking powder
- Food coloring (optional)
- Sprinkles or colored sugar for decorating (optional)

Instructions:

1. Preheat oven to 375°F (190°C). Line baking sheets with parchment paper.
2. In a large bowl, cream together the softened butter and granulated sugar until light and fluffy.
3. Beat in the egg, vanilla extract, and almond extract (if using) until well combined.
4. In a separate bowl, whisk together the flour and baking powder.
5. Gradually add the dry ingredients to the wet ingredients, mixing until a dough forms.
6. If desired, divide the dough into portions and tint each portion with food coloring.
7. Fill a cookie press with the dough, following the manufacturer's instructions for desired shapes.
8. Press the dough onto the prepared baking sheets, spacing cookies about 1 inch apart.
9. Decorate the cookies with sprinkles or colored sugar, if desired.
10. Bake for 8-10 minutes, or until the edges are lightly golden.
11. Let the cookies cool on the baking sheets for a few minutes before transferring them to wire racks to cool completely.
12. Enjoy these festive spritz cookies as a delightful treat or for holiday celebrations!

Red Velvet Cookies

Ingredients:

- 2 1/4 cups all-purpose flour
- 2 tablespoons unsweetened cocoa powder
- 1 teaspoon baking soda
- 1/4 teaspoon salt
- 1/2 cup unsalted butter, softened
- 3/4 cup granulated sugar
- 3/4 cup packed brown sugar
- 2 large eggs
- 1 tablespoon red food coloring
- 1 teaspoon vanilla extract
- 1 cup white chocolate chips or chunks
- Optional: cream cheese frosting for drizzling (see instructions below)

Instructions:

1. Preheat oven to 375°F (190°C). Line baking sheets with parchment paper.
2. In a medium bowl, whisk together the flour, cocoa powder, baking soda, and salt. Set aside.
3. In a large bowl, cream together the softened butter, granulated sugar, and brown sugar until light and fluffy.
4. Beat in the eggs, one at a time, until well combined. Stir in the red food coloring and vanilla extract.
5. Gradually add the dry ingredients to the wet ingredients, mixing until just combined.
6. Fold in the white chocolate chips or chunks until evenly distributed throughout the dough.
7. Drop tablespoon-sized portions of dough onto the prepared baking sheets, spacing them about 2 inches apart.
8. Bake for 8-10 minutes, or until the edges are set and the tops are slightly cracked.
9. Let the cookies cool on the baking sheets for a few minutes before transferring them to wire racks to cool completely.

Optional Cream Cheese Frosting:

- 4 ounces cream cheese, softened
- 1/4 cup unsalted butter, softened

- 1 cup confectioners' sugar
- 1/2 teaspoon vanilla extract

1. In a medium bowl, beat together the softened cream cheese and butter until smooth.
2. Gradually add the confectioners' sugar and vanilla extract, beating until smooth and creamy.
3. Drizzle or spread the cream cheese frosting over the cooled cookies for an extra touch of decadence. Enjoy these vibrant red velvet cookies with a cream cheese frosting drizzle!

Pumpkin Cookies

Ingredients:

- 2 1/2 cups all-purpose flour
- 1 teaspoon baking powder
- 1 teaspoon baking soda
- 1/2 teaspoon salt
- 1 teaspoon ground cinnamon
- 1/2 teaspoon ground ginger
- 1/4 teaspoon ground cloves
- 1/2 cup unsalted butter, softened
- 1 cup granulated sugar
- 1 cup canned pumpkin puree
- 1 large egg
- 1 teaspoon vanilla extract
- Optional: 1 cup chocolate chips, raisins, or chopped nuts

Instructions:

1. Preheat oven to 350°F (175°C). Line baking sheets with parchment paper.
2. In a medium bowl, whisk together the flour, baking powder, baking soda, salt, cinnamon, ginger, and cloves. Set aside.
3. In a large bowl, cream together the softened butter and granulated sugar until light and fluffy.
4. Beat in the pumpkin puree, egg, and vanilla extract until well combined.
5. Gradually add the dry ingredients to the wet ingredients, mixing until just combined.
6. If desired, fold in chocolate chips, raisins, or chopped nuts until evenly distributed throughout the dough.
7. Drop tablespoon-sized portions of dough onto the prepared baking sheets, spacing them about 2 inches apart.
8. Bake for 12-14 minutes, or until the cookies are set and lightly golden around the edges.
9. Let the cookies cool on the baking sheets for a few minutes before transferring them to wire racks to cool completely.
10. Enjoy these delicious pumpkin cookies with a cup of hot cider or your favorite fall beverage!

Toffee Cookies

Ingredients:

- 1 cup unsalted butter, softened
- 1 cup granulated sugar
- 1 cup packed brown sugar
- 2 large eggs
- 1 teaspoon vanilla extract
- 3 cups all-purpose flour
- 1 teaspoon baking soda
- 1/2 teaspoon salt
- 1 1/2 cups toffee bits or chopped toffee candy
- Optional: additional toffee bits for topping

Instructions:

1. Preheat oven to 350°F (175°C). Line baking sheets with parchment paper.
2. In a large bowl, cream together the softened butter, granulated sugar, and brown sugar until light and fluffy.
3. Beat in the eggs, one at a time, until well combined. Stir in the vanilla extract.
4. In a separate bowl, whisk together the flour, baking soda, and salt.
5. Gradually add the dry ingredients to the wet ingredients, mixing until just combined.
6. Fold in the toffee bits until evenly distributed throughout the dough.
7. Drop tablespoon-sized portions of dough onto the prepared baking sheets, spacing them about 2 inches apart.
8. If desired, press a few additional toffee bits onto the tops of each cookie for extra toffee flavor and decoration.
9. Bake for 10-12 minutes, or until the cookies are set and lightly golden around the edges.
10. Let the cookies cool on the baking sheets for a few minutes before transferring them to wire racks to cool completely.
11. Enjoy these delightful toffee cookies with a glass of cold milk or your favorite hot beverage!

Raspberry Bars

Ingredients:

For the Crust:

- 1 1/2 cups all-purpose flour
- 1/2 cup granulated sugar
- 1/4 teaspoon salt
- 3/4 cup unsalted butter, chilled and cubed

For the Raspberry Filling:

- 2 cups fresh raspberries (or thawed frozen raspberries)
- 1/4 cup granulated sugar
- 2 tablespoons cornstarch
- 1 tablespoon lemon juice

Instructions:

1. Preheat the oven to 350°F (175°C). Grease and line an 8x8-inch baking pan with parchment paper, leaving an overhang on the sides for easy removal.
2. Prepare the Crust:
    - In a mixing bowl, whisk together the flour, sugar, and salt.
    - Add the chilled butter cubes and use a pastry cutter or your fingers to cut the butter into the flour mixture until it resembles coarse crumbs and starts to hold together.
    - Press the mixture evenly into the bottom of the prepared baking pan.
    - Bake the crust in the preheated oven for 15-18 minutes, or until lightly golden brown.
3. Prepare the Raspberry Filling:
    - In a saucepan, combine the raspberries, sugar, cornstarch, and lemon juice.
    - Cook over medium heat, stirring constantly, until the mixture thickens and comes to a boil.
    - Reduce the heat to low and continue cooking for another 2-3 minutes, stirring constantly, until the mixture is thick and glossy.
    - Remove from heat and let the raspberry filling cool slightly.
4. Assemble and Bake:
    - Once the crust is baked, pour the raspberry filling over the warm crust, spreading it into an even layer.

- Return the pan to the oven and bake for an additional 20-25 minutes, or until the filling is set.
- Remove from the oven and let the raspberry bars cool completely in the pan on a wire rack.

5. Serve:
    - Once cooled, use the parchment paper overhang to lift the bars out of the pan.
    - Cut into squares or bars and serve. Optionally, dust with powdered sugar before serving for an extra touch.

6. Storage:
    - Store the raspberry bars in an airtight container in the refrigerator for up to 3-4 days. Enjoy chilled or at room temperature.

Lemon Bars

Ingredients:

For the Crust:

- 1 cup all-purpose flour
- 1/4 cup granulated sugar
- 1/2 cup unsalted butter, softened

For the Lemon Filling:

- 1 cup granulated sugar
- 3 tablespoons all-purpose flour
- 1/2 teaspoon baking powder
- 1/4 teaspoon salt
- 2 large eggs
- 1/4 cup lemon juice (about 2-3 lemons)
- Zest of 1 lemon
- Powdered sugar, for dusting (optional)

Instructions:

1. Preheat the oven:
    - Preheat your oven to 350°F (175°C). Grease and line an 8x8-inch baking pan with parchment paper, leaving an overhang on the sides for easy removal.
2. Prepare the Crust:
    - In a mixing bowl, combine the flour, granulated sugar, and softened butter.
    - Use a fork or pastry cutter to mix until crumbly and the dough starts to come together.
    - Press the dough evenly into the bottom of the prepared baking pan.
3. Bake the Crust:
    - Place the pan in the preheated oven and bake the crust for 15-18 minutes, or until lightly golden brown.
4. Prepare the Lemon Filling:
    - In another mixing bowl, whisk together the granulated sugar, flour, baking powder, and salt.
    - Add the eggs, lemon juice, and lemon zest to the dry ingredients and whisk until smooth and well combined.
5. Assemble and Bake:

- Once the crust is baked, pour the lemon filling over the warm crust, spreading it into an even layer.
 - Return the pan to the oven and bake for an additional 20-25 minutes, or until the filling is set and the edges are lightly golden brown.
6. Cool and Serve:
 - Remove the pan from the oven and let the lemon bars cool completely in the pan on a wire rack.
 - Once cooled, use the parchment paper overhang to lift the bars out of the pan.
 - Cut into squares or bars. Optionally, dust with powdered sugar before serving for an extra touch.
7. Storage:
 - Store the lemon bars in an airtight container in the refrigerator for up to 3-4 days. Enjoy chilled or at room temperature.

Brownies

Ingredients:

- 1 cup (2 sticks) unsalted butter
- 2 cups granulated sugar
- 4 large eggs
- 1 teaspoon vanilla extract
- 1 cup all-purpose flour
- 3/4 cup unsweetened cocoa powder
- 1/2 teaspoon salt
- Optional: 1 cup chopped nuts or chocolate chips

Instructions:

1. Preheat your oven to 350°F (175°C). Grease a 9x13-inch baking pan or line it with parchment paper.
2. In a medium saucepan, melt the butter over low heat. Remove from heat and stir in the sugar until well combined.
3. Add the eggs, one at a time, mixing well after each addition. Stir in the vanilla extract.
4. In a separate bowl, sift together the flour, cocoa powder, and salt. Gradually add the dry ingredients to the wet ingredients, mixing until just combined.
5. If desired, fold in the chopped nuts or chocolate chips until evenly distributed throughout the batter.
6. Pour the batter into the prepared baking pan and spread it out evenly with a spatula.
7. Bake in the preheated oven for 25-30 minutes, or until a toothpick inserted into the center comes out with moist crumbs, but not wet batter.
8. Remove the brownies from the oven and let them cool completely in the pan on a wire rack.
9. Once cooled, cut into squares and serve. Enjoy your delicious homemade brownies! Optional: Dust with powdered sugar or drizzle with melted chocolate for extra indulgence.

Blondies

Ingredients:

- 1 cup (2 sticks) unsalted butter, melted
- 2 cups packed light brown sugar
- 2 large eggs
- 1 tablespoon vanilla extract
- 2 cups all-purpose flour
- 1 teaspoon baking powder
- 1/2 teaspoon salt
- 1 cup white chocolate chips or chunks
- 1 cup chopped nuts (such as pecans or walnuts), optional

Instructions:

1. Preheat your oven to 350°F (175°C). Grease a 9x13-inch baking pan or line it with parchment paper.
2. In a large mixing bowl, whisk together the melted butter and brown sugar until well combined.
3. Beat in the eggs, one at a time, until smooth. Stir in the vanilla extract.
4. In a separate bowl, sift together the flour, baking powder, and salt. Gradually add the dry ingredients to the wet ingredients, mixing until just combined.
5. Fold in the white chocolate chips or chunks and chopped nuts (if using) until evenly distributed throughout the batter.
6. Pour the batter into the prepared baking pan and spread it out evenly with a spatula.
7. Bake in the preheated oven for 25-30 minutes, or until the blondies are set and lightly golden brown around the edges.
8. Remove the blondies from the oven and let them cool completely in the pan on a wire rack.
9. Once cooled, cut into squares or bars and serve. Enjoy your delicious homemade blondies! Optional: Dust with powdered sugar or drizzle with melted white chocolate for extra indulgence.

Magic Cookie Bars

Ingredients:

- 1/2 cup (1 stick) unsalted butter, melted
- 1 1/2 cups graham cracker crumbs
- 1 cup semisweet chocolate chips
- 1 cup butterscotch chips
- 1 cup shredded coconut
- 1 cup chopped nuts (such as walnuts or pecans)
- 1 (14-ounce) can sweetened condensed milk

Instructions:

1. Preheat your oven to 350°F (175°C). Grease a 9x13-inch baking pan or line it with parchment paper.
2. In a medium bowl, mix the melted butter and graham cracker crumbs until well combined. Press the mixture evenly into the bottom of the prepared baking pan.
3. Sprinkle the semisweet chocolate chips, butterscotch chips, shredded coconut, and chopped nuts evenly over the graham cracker crust.
4. Pour the sweetened condensed milk evenly over the top of the layers.
5. Bake in the preheated oven for 25-30 minutes, or until the edges are lightly golden brown and the top is set.
6. Remove the pan from the oven and let the magic cookie bars cool completely in the pan on a wire rack.
7. Once cooled, cut into squares or bars and serve. Enjoy your delicious homemade magic cookie bars! These bars can be stored in an airtight container at room temperature for several days.

Rice Krispie Treats

Ingredients:

- 6 cups crispy rice cereal (such as Rice Krispies)
- 4 cups miniature marshmallows
- 3 tablespoons unsalted butter

Instructions:

1. Grease a 9x13-inch baking pan or line it with parchment paper.
2. In a large saucepan, melt the butter over low heat.
3. Add the miniature marshmallows to the melted butter and stir continuously until the marshmallows are completely melted and smooth.
4. Remove the saucepan from heat and quickly stir in the crispy rice cereal until it is evenly coated with the melted marshmallow mixture.
5. Transfer the mixture to the prepared baking pan and use a greased spatula or your hands to press it down firmly into an even layer.
6. Let the Rice Krispie treats cool and set in the pan for at least 30 minutes.
7. Once cooled and set, cut the Rice Krispie treats into squares or bars using a sharp knife.
8. Serve and enjoy these classic homemade treats! They can be stored in an airtight container at room temperature for several days.

Fudge

Ingredients:

- 3 cups semisweet chocolate chips
- 1 (14-ounce) can sweetened condensed milk
- 1/4 cup unsalted butter
- 1 teaspoon vanilla extract
- Optional: chopped nuts, marshmallows, or other mix-ins

Instructions:

1. Grease an 8x8-inch baking pan or line it with parchment paper, leaving an overhang on the sides for easy removal.
2. In a medium saucepan, combine the semisweet chocolate chips, sweetened condensed milk, and unsalted butter.
3. Place the saucepan over low heat and stir continuously until the chocolate chips are melted and the mixture is smooth and well combined. Be careful not to let it burn.
4. Once the mixture is smooth, remove the saucepan from the heat and stir in the vanilla extract.
5. If desired, fold in chopped nuts, marshmallows, or other mix-ins until evenly distributed throughout the fudge mixture.
6. Pour the fudge mixture into the prepared baking pan and spread it out evenly with a spatula.
7. Let the fudge cool and set at room temperature for at least 2 hours, or until firm.
8. Once the fudge is set, use the parchment paper overhang to lift it out of the pan. Cut the fudge into squares or bars using a sharp knife.
9. Serve and enjoy your homemade chocolate fudge! Store any leftovers in an airtight container at room temperature for several days.

Peanut Butter Bars

Ingredients:

For the Base:

- 1/2 cup (1 stick) unsalted butter, melted
- 2 cups graham cracker crumbs
- 1 cup powdered sugar
- 1 cup creamy peanut butter

For the Topping:

- 1 1/2 cups semisweet chocolate chips
- 1/4 cup creamy peanut butter

Instructions:

1. Grease a 9x13-inch baking pan or line it with parchment paper, leaving an overhang on the sides for easy removal.
2. In a medium bowl, mix together the melted butter, graham cracker crumbs, powdered sugar, and creamy peanut butter until well combined.
3. Press the mixture evenly into the bottom of the prepared baking pan to form the base layer.
4. In a microwave-safe bowl, combine the semisweet chocolate chips and creamy peanut butter for the topping. Microwave in 30-second intervals, stirring in between, until the mixture is melted and smooth.
5. Pour the melted chocolate and peanut butter mixture over the peanut butter base layer in the baking pan, spreading it out evenly with a spatula.
6. Refrigerate the pan for at least 1 hour, or until the chocolate topping is set.
7. Once set, remove the pan from the refrigerator and let it sit at room temperature for a few minutes to soften slightly.
8. Use a sharp knife to cut the bars into squares or bars.
9. Serve and enjoy your delicious homemade peanut butter bars! Store any leftovers in an airtight container in the refrigerator for up to one week.

S'mores Bars

Ingredients:

For the Graham Cracker Crust:

- 2 cups graham cracker crumbs
- 1/2 cup unsalted butter, melted
- 1/4 cup granulated sugar

For the Chocolate Layer:

- 2 cups semisweet chocolate chips

For the Marshmallow Layer:

- 3 cups mini marshmallows

For Topping:

- 1 cup graham cracker pieces
- 1/2 cup semisweet chocolate chips, for drizzling (optional)

Instructions:

1. Preheat your oven to 350°F (175°C). Grease a 9x13-inch baking pan or line it with parchment paper, leaving an overhang on the sides for easy removal.
2. Prepare the Graham Cracker Crust:
    - In a mixing bowl, combine the graham cracker crumbs, melted butter, and granulated sugar until well combined.
    - Press the mixture evenly into the bottom of the prepared baking pan to form the crust layer.
3. Bake the Crust:
    - Place the pan in the preheated oven and bake the crust for 8-10 minutes, or until lightly golden brown.
    - Remove from the oven and let it cool slightly.
4. Add the Chocolate Layer:
    - Sprinkle the semisweet chocolate chips evenly over the warm graham cracker crust.
    - Return the pan to the oven for 2-3 minutes, or until the chocolate chips are softened.

- Use a spatula to spread the softened chocolate chips into an even layer over the crust.
5. Add the Marshmallow Layer:
   - Sprinkle the mini marshmallows evenly over the melted chocolate layer.
6. Bake Again:
   - Return the pan to the oven and bake for an additional 5-7 minutes, or until the marshmallows are puffed and lightly golden brown.
7. Cool and Garnish:
   - Remove the pan from the oven and let the s'mores bars cool completely in the pan on a wire rack.
   - Once cooled, sprinkle the graham cracker pieces over the marshmallow layer.
   - If desired, melt the remaining 1/2 cup of chocolate chips and drizzle over the top of the bars for extra chocolatey goodness.
8. Cut and Serve:
   - Once completely cooled and set, use a sharp knife to cut the s'mores bars into squares or bars.
   - Serve and enjoy your delicious homemade s'mores bars! Store any leftovers in an airtight container at room temperature.

Caramel Corn

Ingredients:

- 12 cups popped popcorn (about 1/2 cup unpopped kernels)
- 1 cup unsalted butter
- 2 cups packed brown sugar
- 1/2 cup light corn syrup
- 1 teaspoon salt
- 1/2 teaspoon baking soda
- 1 teaspoon vanilla extract

Instructions:

1. Preheat your oven to 250°F (120°C). Line two large baking sheets with parchment paper or silicone baking mats.
2. Place the popped popcorn in a large mixing bowl, making sure to remove any unpopped kernels.
3. In a medium saucepan, melt the butter over medium heat. Stir in the brown sugar, corn syrup, and salt.
4. Bring the mixture to a boil, stirring constantly. Once boiling, let it cook without stirring for 4-5 minutes.
5. Remove the saucepan from heat and stir in the baking soda and vanilla extract. The mixture will foam up.
6. Pour the hot caramel sauce over the popcorn in the mixing bowl. Use a spatula or wooden spoon to gently toss the popcorn until evenly coated with the caramel.
7. Divide the caramel-coated popcorn between the prepared baking sheets, spreading it out into an even layer.
8. Bake the caramel corn in the preheated oven for 45-60 minutes, stirring every 15 minutes to ensure even coating.
9. Remove the baking sheets from the oven and let the caramel corn cool completely on the pans.
10. Once cooled, break the caramel corn into clusters or pieces and transfer to an airtight container for storage.
11. Enjoy your homemade caramel corn as a delicious snack! It can be stored at room temperature for up to a week.

Chocolate Bark

Ingredients:

- 16 ounces (about 450g) of high-quality chocolate (dark, milk, or white chocolate)
- Toppings of your choice:
    - Chopped nuts (almonds, pecans, pistachios, etc.)
    - Dried fruits (cranberries, apricots, cherries, etc.)
    - Crushed cookies or graham crackers
    - Coconut flakes
    - Sea salt
    - Sprinkles
    - Crushed candy canes (for a festive touch)

Instructions:

1. Line a baking sheet with parchment paper or a silicone baking mat.
2. Chop the chocolate into small, uniform pieces for even melting.
3. In a microwave-safe bowl, microwave the chocolate in 30-second intervals, stirring after each interval, until melted and smooth. Alternatively, you can melt the chocolate using a double boiler.
4. Once the chocolate is melted, pour it onto the prepared baking sheet. Use a spatula or the back of a spoon to spread the chocolate into an even layer, about 1/4 to 1/2 inch thick.
5. Immediately sprinkle your desired toppings over the melted chocolate. You can be as creative as you like with the toppings, covering the entire surface evenly.
6. If desired, sprinkle a pinch of sea salt over the top for a sweet and salty flavor contrast.
7. Place the baking sheet in the refrigerator for about 30 minutes, or until the chocolate is completely set and firm.
8. Once set, break the chocolate bark into pieces of your desired size and shape using your hands or a sharp knife.
9. Serve and enjoy your homemade chocolate bark! Store any leftovers in an airtight container at room temperature or in the refrigerator for up to two weeks.

Whoopie Pies

Ingredients:

For the Chocolate Whoopie Pie Cakes:

- 2 cups all-purpose flour
- 1/2 cup unsweetened cocoa powder
- 1 teaspoon baking powder
- 1 teaspoon baking soda
- 1/2 teaspoon salt
- 1/2 cup unsalted butter, softened
- 1 cup granulated sugar
- 1 large egg
- 1 teaspoon vanilla extract
- 1 cup buttermilk

For the Filling:

- 1/2 cup unsalted butter, softened
- 1 cup powdered sugar
- 1 teaspoon vanilla extract
- 1 1/2 cups marshmallow fluff or marshmallow cream

Instructions:

1. Preheat your oven to 350°F (175°C). Line baking sheets with parchment paper.
2. In a medium bowl, whisk together the flour, cocoa powder, baking powder, baking soda, and salt. Set aside.
3. In a large bowl, cream together the softened butter and granulated sugar until light and fluffy.
4. Beat in the egg and vanilla extract until well combined.
5. Gradually add the dry ingredients to the wet ingredients, alternating with the buttermilk, beginning and ending with the dry ingredients. Mix until just combined.
6. Drop tablespoon-sized portions of batter onto the prepared baking sheets, spacing them about 2 inches apart.
7. Bake for 10-12 minutes, or until the cakes spring back when lightly touched.
8. Remove from the oven and let the cakes cool on the baking sheets for a few minutes before transferring them to wire racks to cool completely.

9. While the cakes are cooling, prepare the filling. In a medium bowl, beat together the softened butter, powdered sugar, and vanilla extract until smooth and creamy.
10. Fold in the marshmallow fluff until evenly combined.
11. Once the cakes are completely cooled, spread a generous amount of filling onto the flat side of half of the cakes. Top with the remaining cakes to form sandwiches.
12. Serve and enjoy your delicious homemade whoopie pies! Store any leftovers in an airtight container in the refrigerator.

Macarons

Ingredients:

For the Macaron Shells:

- 1 cup (100g) almond flour
- 1 3/4 cups (200g) powdered sugar
- 3 large egg whites, room temperature
- 1/4 cup (50g) granulated sugar
- Gel food coloring (optional)

For the Filling:

- Your choice of filling (e.g., buttercream, ganache, jam)

Instructions:

1. Prepare Baking Sheets: Line two baking sheets with parchment paper or silicone baking mats.
2. Prepare Almond Mixture: In a medium bowl, sift together the almond flour and powdered sugar. Set aside.
3. Whip Egg Whites: In a clean, dry mixing bowl, beat the egg whites on medium speed until foamy. Gradually add the granulated sugar, increase the speed to medium-high, and continue beating until stiff peaks form. If using food coloring, add a few drops at this stage.
4. Macaronage: Gently fold the almond mixture into the whipped egg whites using a spatula until just combined. Be careful not to overmix; the batter should flow like lava and ribbons should disappear into the batter after about 10 seconds.
5. Pipe Macarons: Transfer the batter to a piping bag fitted with a round tip. Pipe small rounds onto the prepared baking sheets, leaving space between each macaron.
6. Rest and Preheat Oven: Tap the baking sheets firmly on the counter to release any air bubbles, then let the macarons sit at room temperature for 30-60 minutes, until a skin forms on the surface. Preheat your oven to 300°F (150°C).
7. Bake Macarons: Bake the macarons in the preheated oven for 15-18 minutes, until set and the tops are firm to the touch. Let them cool completely on the baking sheets.
8. Fill Macarons: Once cooled, pair up the macaron shells based on size. Pipe or spread a small amount of filling onto the flat side of one shell, then sandwich with another shell.

9. Mature Macarons: Place the filled macarons in an airtight container and refrigerate for 24-48 hours to mature. Bring to room temperature before serving.
10. Serve: Enjoy your homemade macarons as a delightful treat!

Feel free to experiment with different flavors and fillings to create your own unique macarons!

Madeleines

Ingredients:

- 2/3 cup (135g) granulated sugar
- 3 large eggs, room temperature
- 1 teaspoon vanilla extract
- 1/8 teaspoon salt
- 1 cup (125g) all-purpose flour
- 1 teaspoon baking powder
- 10 tablespoons (140g) unsalted butter, melted and cooled, plus extra for greasing the pans
- Powdered sugar, for dusting (optional)

Instructions:

1. Prepare Madeleine Pans: Preheat your oven to 350°F (175°C). Brush the madeleine molds with melted butter and lightly flour them, tapping out any excess flour.
2. Whisk Eggs and Sugar: In a large mixing bowl, whisk together the eggs, granulated sugar, vanilla extract, and salt until pale and thickened, about 5 minutes.
3. Sift Dry Ingredients: In a separate bowl, sift together the all-purpose flour and baking powder.
4. Fold in Dry Ingredients: Gradually fold the sifted dry ingredients into the egg mixture until just combined.
5. Add Melted Butter: Gently fold in the melted and cooled butter until fully incorporated into the batter.
6. Chill Batter: Cover the bowl with plastic wrap and refrigerate the batter for at least 30 minutes, or up to overnight.
7. Fill Madeleine Molds: Drop spoonfuls of the chilled batter into each prepared madeleine mold, filling each about 3/4 full.
8. Bake: Bake the madeleines in the preheated oven for 10-12 minutes, or until the edges are golden brown and the tops spring back when lightly touched.
9. Cool and Serve: Remove the madeleine pans from the oven and let them cool for a few minutes before carefully transferring the madeleines to a wire rack to cool completely.
10. Optional: Dust the cooled madeleines with powdered sugar before serving for a decorative touch.

11. Serve: Enjoy your homemade madeleines with a cup of tea or coffee as a delightful snack or dessert! They are best enjoyed the day they are made but can be stored in an airtight container at room temperature for up to 2 days.

Biscotti

Ingredients:

- 2 cups (250g) all-purpose flour
- 1 cup (200g) granulated sugar
- 1 teaspoon baking powder
- 1/4 teaspoon salt
- 3 large eggs
- 1 teaspoon vanilla extract
- 1 teaspoon almond extract
- 1 cup (125g) whole almonds, toasted and chopped

Instructions:

1. Preheat Oven: Preheat your oven to 350°F (175°C). Line a baking sheet with parchment paper or a silicone baking mat.
2. Prepare Dry Ingredients: In a large mixing bowl, whisk together the all-purpose flour, granulated sugar, baking powder, and salt until well combined.
3. Mix Wet Ingredients: In a separate bowl, beat the eggs together with the vanilla extract and almond extract until well blended.
4. Combine Wet and Dry Ingredients: Gradually add the wet ingredients to the dry ingredients, mixing until a dough forms. Fold in the chopped almonds until evenly distributed throughout the dough.
5. Shape Dough: Transfer the dough to a lightly floured surface and divide it into two equal portions. Shape each portion into a log about 12 inches long and 2 inches wide. Place the logs on the prepared baking sheet, spacing them a few inches apart.
6. Bake: Bake the biscotti logs in the preheated oven for 25-30 minutes, or until firm to the touch and lightly golden brown.
7. Cool: Remove the baking sheet from the oven and let the biscotti logs cool for about 10 minutes.
8. Slice Biscotti: Using a sharp knife, carefully slice the biscotti logs diagonally into 1/2-inch thick slices.
9. Second Bake: Arrange the sliced biscotti cut-side down on the baking sheet and return them to the oven. Bake for an additional 10-12 minutes, or until the biscotti are crisp and lightly golden brown.
10. Cool and Serve: Remove the biscotti from the oven and let them cool completely on a wire rack. Once cooled, store the biscotti in an airtight container at room temperature.

11. Serve: Enjoy your homemade almond biscotti with a cup of coffee or tea for a delightful treat! They also make great gifts when packaged in decorative bags or boxes.

Rocky Road

Ingredients:

- 1/2 cup (1 stick) unsalted butter
- 12 ounces (about 2 cups) semisweet chocolate chips
- 1/4 cup unsweetened cocoa powder
- 1/4 cup granulated sugar
- 1 teaspoon vanilla extract
- 2 large eggs
- 1 1/4 cups all-purpose flour
- 1/4 teaspoon salt
- 1 cup mini marshmallows
- 1/2 cup chopped nuts (such as walnuts or almonds)
- 1/2 cup chopped chocolate or chocolate chunks

Instructions:

1. Preheat Oven: Preheat your oven to 350°F (175°C). Grease or line an 8x8-inch baking pan with parchment paper.
2. Melt Chocolate: In a medium saucepan, melt the butter and semisweet chocolate chips over low heat, stirring constantly until smooth. Remove from heat and let cool slightly.
3. Mix Wet Ingredients: Stir in the cocoa powder, granulated sugar, vanilla extract, and eggs until well combined.
4. Add Dry Ingredients: Gradually add the flour and salt, stirring until just combined. Do not overmix.
5. Fold in Add-ins: Gently fold in the mini marshmallows, chopped nuts, and chopped chocolate until evenly distributed throughout the batter.
6. Bake: Pour the batter into the prepared baking pan and spread it out evenly with a spatula. Bake in the preheated oven for 25-30 minutes, or until a toothpick inserted into the center comes out with moist crumbs.
7. Cool: Remove the pan from the oven and let the bars cool completely in the pan on a wire rack.
8. Slice and Serve: Once cooled, use a sharp knife to cut the rocky road bars into squares. Serve and enjoy these delicious homemade treats!
9. Storage: Store any leftover rocky road bars in an airtight container at room temperature for up to 3-4 days. They can also be stored in the refrigerator for longer freshness.

Marshmallow Treats

Ingredients:

- 6 cups crispy rice cereal (such as Rice Krispies)
- 1/4 cup (1/2 stick) unsalted butter
- 1 package (10 ounces) marshmallows (about 40 marshmallows)
- Optional: additional marshmallows for topping

Instructions:

1. Prepare Pan: Grease a 9x13-inch baking pan or line it with parchment paper.
2. Melt Butter: In a large pot or saucepan, melt the butter over low heat.
3. Add Marshmallows: Once the butter is melted, add the marshmallows to the pot. Stir continuously until the marshmallows are completely melted and the mixture is smooth.
4. Add Cereal: Remove the pot from the heat and quickly add the crispy rice cereal to the melted marshmallow mixture. Stir until the cereal is evenly coated with the marshmallow mixture.
5. Press into Pan: Transfer the mixture to the prepared baking pan. Use a greased spatula or your hands (lightly greased with butter or cooking spray) to press the mixture firmly and evenly into the pan.
6. Optional Topping: If desired, press additional marshmallows onto the top of the treats for decoration.
7. Cool and Cut: Let the marshmallow treats cool and set in the pan for at least 30 minutes.
8. Slice and Serve: Once cooled and set, cut the treats into squares or rectangles using a sharp knife. Serve and enjoy!
9. Storage: Store any leftover marshmallow treats in an airtight container at room temperature for up to several days.

Truffles

Ingredients:

- 8 ounces (about 227g) high-quality semisweet or bittersweet chocolate, finely chopped
- 1/2 cup (120ml) heavy cream
- 1 tablespoon unsalted butter, at room temperature
- 1 teaspoon vanilla extract
- Optional coatings:
  - Cocoa powder
  - Chopped nuts (such as almonds, hazelnuts, or pistachios)
  - Shredded coconut
  - Powdered sugar
  - Melted chocolate for dipping

Instructions:

1. Prepare Chocolate: Place the finely chopped chocolate in a heatproof bowl.
2. Heat Cream: In a small saucepan, heat the heavy cream over medium heat until it just begins to simmer. Remove from heat immediately.
3. Combine Cream and Chocolate: Pour the hot cream over the chopped chocolate. Let it sit for 1-2 minutes to soften the chocolate. Then, gently stir until the chocolate is completely melted and the mixture is smooth.
4. Add Butter and Vanilla: Stir in the unsalted butter and vanilla extract until well combined and smooth.
5. Chill Mixture: Cover the bowl with plastic wrap and refrigerate the chocolate mixture for at least 2 hours, or until firm enough to handle.
6. Shape Truffles: Once chilled, use a spoon or a small scoop to portion out the chocolate mixture. Roll each portion into a smooth ball between the palms of your hands. Place the rolled truffles on a baking sheet lined with parchment paper.
7. Coat Truffles: Roll the truffles in your desired coatings (cocoa powder, chopped nuts, shredded coconut, powdered sugar, etc.) until evenly coated. Place the coated truffles back on the baking sheet.
8. Optional: Dip in Chocolate: If desired, melt some additional chocolate and dip the coated truffles into the melted chocolate. Use a fork to lift the truffles out of the chocolate, tapping off any excess, and place them back on the baking sheet.
9. Chill Again (Optional): Once all the truffles are coated and dipped, refrigerate them for about 15-30 minutes to set the coatings.

10. Serve: Serve the chocolate truffles at room temperature for the best texture and flavor. Enjoy!
11. Storage: Store the chocolate truffles in an airtight container in the refrigerator for up to 2 weeks. Bring them to room temperature before serving.

Chocolate-Covered Pretzels

Ingredients:

- Pretzels (any shape or size)
- 8 ounces (about 227g) high-quality chocolate (dark, milk, or white), chopped
- Toppings of your choice (optional):
    - Sprinkles
    - Chopped nuts (such as almonds, peanuts, or pecans)
    - Shredded coconut
    - Crushed candy canes
    - Sea salt

Instructions:

1. Prepare Baking Sheet: Line a baking sheet with parchment paper or a silicone baking mat.
2. Melt Chocolate: Place the chopped chocolate in a heatproof bowl. Microwave in 30-second intervals, stirring in between, until melted and smooth. Alternatively, melt the chocolate using a double boiler.
3. Dip Pretzels: Dip each pretzel into the melted chocolate, using a fork or a dipping tool to fully coat it. Allow any excess chocolate to drip off.
4. Place on Baking Sheet: Place the chocolate-covered pretzels on the prepared baking sheet, spacing them apart to prevent sticking.
5. Add Toppings (Optional): If desired, sprinkle the toppings of your choice over the chocolate-covered pretzels before the chocolate sets. Be sure to do this while the chocolate is still wet so that the toppings adhere.
6. Let Set: Allow the chocolate-covered pretzels to set at room temperature until the chocolate hardens. You can also place them in the refrigerator for faster setting.
7. Serve or Store: Once the chocolate is fully set, serve the chocolate-covered pretzels as a delicious snack or dessert. Store any leftovers in an airtight container at room temperature for several days.
8. Enjoy: Enjoy your homemade chocolate-covered pretzels as a sweet and salty treat! They're perfect for parties, gatherings, or simply as a tasty snack anytime.

Caramel Apples

Ingredients:

- 6-8 medium-sized apples (Granny Smith or any firm variety)
- 1 (14-ounce) package soft caramel candies
- 2 tablespoons heavy cream or milk
- Wooden sticks or skewers
- Toppings of your choice (optional):
    - Chopped nuts (such as peanuts, almonds, or pecans)
    - Mini chocolate chips
    - Sprinkles
    - Crushed cookies (such as Oreos)
    - Sea salt

Instructions:

1. Prepare Apples: Wash and thoroughly dry the apples. Remove any stems and insert wooden sticks or skewers into the stem end of each apple. Set aside.
2. Melt Caramel: Unwrap the individual caramel candies and place them in a microwave-safe bowl along with the heavy cream or milk. Microwave in 30-second intervals, stirring in between, until the caramels are completely melted and smooth. Alternatively, melt the caramels with cream in a saucepan over low heat, stirring constantly.
3. Dip Apples: Hold each apple by the wooden stick and dip it into the melted caramel, swirling and rotating to coat the entire apple evenly. Allow any excess caramel to drip off.
4. Add Toppings (Optional): If desired, immediately roll the caramel-coated apples in your choice of toppings, gently pressing them onto the caramel to adhere. You can also drizzle melted chocolate over the caramel-coated apples for extra indulgence.
5. Let Set: Place the caramel apples on a parchment-lined baking sheet or wax paper to set. You can refrigerate them briefly to speed up the setting process.
6. Serve or Store: Once the caramel is set, serve the caramel apples immediately or wrap them individually in plastic wrap for storage. Enjoy your homemade caramel apples as a delicious fall treat!
7. Note: Caramel apples are best enjoyed the same day they are made. If storing, keep them in the refrigerator and bring them to room temperature before serving for the best taste and texture.

Peanut Brittle

Ingredients:

- 1 cup granulated sugar
- 1/2 cup light corn syrup
- 1/4 cup water
- 1 cup raw peanuts (unsalted)
- 1 tablespoon unsalted butter
- 1 teaspoon vanilla extract
- 1 teaspoon baking soda

Instructions:

1. Prepare Baking Sheet: Line a baking sheet with parchment paper or a silicone baking mat. Set aside.
2. Combine Sugar, Corn Syrup, and Water: In a medium saucepan, combine the granulated sugar, light corn syrup, and water. Stir together over medium heat until the sugar is dissolved.
3. Cook Sugar Mixture: Once the sugar is dissolved, bring the mixture to a boil without stirring. Attach a candy thermometer to the side of the saucepan and continue to cook until the temperature reaches 300°F (hard crack stage). This usually takes about 5-7 minutes.
4. Add Peanuts and Butter: Once the sugar mixture reaches 300°F, carefully stir in the raw peanuts and unsalted butter. Stir continuously until the peanuts are evenly coated with the caramelized sugar mixture.
5. Continue Cooking: Cook the peanut mixture, stirring constantly, until it reaches a deep golden brown color, which usually takes about 3-5 minutes.
6. Remove from Heat and Add Vanilla: Once the peanut mixture is caramelized to your liking, remove the saucepan from the heat. Stir in the vanilla extract until well combined.
7. Add Baking Soda: Quickly stir in the baking soda until it is evenly incorporated into the mixture. The mixture will foam up slightly.
8. Spread onto Baking Sheet: Immediately pour the hot peanut brittle mixture onto the prepared baking sheet. Use a spatula or spoon to spread it out into an even layer, about 1/4 inch thick.
9. Let Cool: Allow the peanut brittle to cool completely at room temperature until hardened, which usually takes about 30-60 minutes.
10. Break into Pieces: Once cooled and hardened, break the peanut brittle into pieces of your desired size using your hands or a knife.

11. Serve or Store: Serve the homemade peanut brittle as a delicious sweet treat. Store any leftovers in an airtight container at room temperature for up to two weeks.

Enjoy your homemade peanut brittle! It's perfect for snacking or gifting during the holiday season.

Nougat

Ingredients:

- 1 cup granulated sugar
- 1/2 cup light corn syrup
- 1/4 cup water
- 2 large egg whites, at room temperature
- Pinch of salt
- 1 teaspoon vanilla extract
- 1 cup chopped nuts (such as almonds, hazelnuts, or pistachios)
- 1 cup chopped dried fruits (such as apricots, cherries, or cranberries)
- Powdered sugar, for dusting

Instructions:

1. Prepare Pan: Line an 8x8-inch baking pan with parchment paper, leaving an overhang on the sides for easy removal. Dust the parchment paper lightly with powdered sugar.
2. Cook Sugar Mixture: In a medium saucepan, combine the granulated sugar, light corn syrup, and water. Stir together over medium heat until the sugar is dissolved.
3. Cook to Soft Ball Stage: Attach a candy thermometer to the side of the saucepan. Cook the sugar mixture, without stirring, until it reaches 240°F (soft ball stage). This usually takes about 8-10 minutes.
4. Whip Egg Whites: While the sugar mixture is cooking, in a clean mixing bowl, beat the egg whites and salt until stiff peaks form.
5. Combine Mixtures: Once the sugar mixture reaches 240°F, remove it from the heat. With the mixer running on low speed, slowly pour the hot sugar mixture into the beaten egg whites in a thin stream, aiming for the side of the bowl to avoid splattering.
6. Whip Mixture: Increase the mixer speed to high and continue beating the mixture until it is thick, glossy, and holds its shape, about 5-7 minutes. Add the vanilla extract during the last minute of mixing.
7. Fold in Nuts and Fruits: Gently fold in the chopped nuts and dried fruits until evenly distributed throughout the nougat mixture.
8. Transfer to Pan: Quickly transfer the nougat mixture to the prepared baking pan, spreading it out into an even layer with a spatula.
9. Let Set: Allow the nougat to cool and set at room temperature for at least 4 hours, or until firm.

10. Cut into Pieces: Once set, lift the nougat out of the pan using the parchment paper overhang. Place it on a cutting board and use a sharp knife to cut it into small squares or rectangles.
11. Dust with Powdered Sugar: Dust the cut nougat pieces lightly with powdered sugar to prevent sticking.
12. Serve or Store: Serve the homemade nougat immediately, or store it in an airtight container at room temperature for up to two weeks.

Enjoy your homemade nougat with its delightful combination of nuts, fruits, and fluffy texture!

Pecan Pralines

Ingredients:

- 1 cup granulated sugar
- 1 cup packed light brown sugar
- 1/2 cup heavy cream
- 2 tablespoons unsalted butter
- 1 1/2 cups pecan halves
- 1 teaspoon vanilla extract
- Pinch of salt

Instructions:

1. Prepare Baking Sheet: Line a baking sheet with parchment paper or a silicone baking mat. Set aside.
2. Cook Sugar Mixture: In a medium saucepan, combine the granulated sugar, brown sugar, heavy cream, and unsalted butter over medium heat. Stir until the sugars are dissolved and the mixture comes to a boil.
3. Cook to Soft Ball Stage: Attach a candy thermometer to the side of the saucepan. Cook the sugar mixture, without stirring, until it reaches 240°F (soft ball stage). This usually takes about 8-10 minutes.
4. Add Pecans: Once the mixture reaches 240°F, remove it from the heat and stir in the pecan halves, vanilla extract, and a pinch of salt.
5. Drop onto Baking Sheet: Quickly drop spoonfuls of the hot pecan praline mixture onto the prepared baking sheet, leaving some space between each praline to allow them to spread.
6. Let Cool: Allow the pecan pralines to cool and set at room temperature for about 20-30 minutes, or until firm.
7. Serve or Store: Once set, serve the homemade pecan pralines immediately, or store them in an airtight container at room temperature for up to one week.
8. Enjoy: Enjoy your homemade pecan pralines as a sweet and nutty treat!

These pecan pralines are perfect for sharing with friends and family or for indulging in as a special treat for yourself.

Chocolate-Covered Cherries

Ingredients:

- Maraschino cherries with stems, drained and patted dry
- 8 ounces (about 227g) high-quality chocolate (dark, milk, or white), chopped
- Optional: 1 tablespoon coconut oil or vegetable shortening (for thinning chocolate)
- Optional: Additional toppings such as sprinkles, chopped nuts, or shredded coconut

Instructions:

1. Prepare Cherries: Drain the maraschino cherries and pat them dry with paper towels. Make sure the cherries are completely dry before dipping them in chocolate to prevent the chocolate from seizing.
2. Melt Chocolate: Place the chopped chocolate in a heatproof bowl. Microwave in 30-second intervals, stirring in between, until melted and smooth. Alternatively, melt the chocolate using a double boiler.
3. Thin Chocolate (Optional): If the melted chocolate is too thick for dipping, stir in 1 tablespoon of coconut oil or vegetable shortening until smooth and thinned to your desired consistency.
4. Dip Cherries: Hold each cherry by the stem and dip it into the melted chocolate, swirling to coat it evenly. Allow any excess chocolate to drip off.
5. Place on Parchment: Place the chocolate-covered cherries on a parchment-lined baking sheet, making sure they are not touching each other.
6. Add Toppings (Optional): If desired, sprinkle additional toppings such as sprinkles, chopped nuts, or shredded coconut over the chocolate-covered cherries before the chocolate sets.
7. Let Set: Allow the chocolate-covered cherries to set at room temperature until the chocolate hardens, which usually takes about 30-60 minutes.
8. Serve or Store: Once the chocolate is fully set, serve the homemade chocolate-covered cherries as a delicious treat. Store any leftovers in an airtight container in the refrigerator for up to one week.
9. Enjoy: Enjoy your homemade chocolate-covered cherries as a delightful combination of sweet fruit and rich chocolate! They're perfect for sharing or for indulging in as a special treat.

Fruitcake Cookies

Ingredients:

- 1 cup chopped mixed dried fruits (such as raisins, currants, cherries, and apricots)
- 1/4 cup brandy or rum (optional)
- 1 cup all-purpose flour
- 1/2 teaspoon baking powder
- 1/4 teaspoon baking soda
- 1/4 teaspoon salt
- 1/2 cup unsalted butter, softened
- 1/2 cup packed brown sugar
- 1 large egg
- 1 teaspoon vanilla extract
- 1/2 cup chopped nuts (such as pecans or walnuts)

Instructions:

1. Preheat Oven: Preheat your oven to 350°F (175°C). Line baking sheets with parchment paper or silicone baking mats.
2. Soak Dried Fruits (Optional): In a small bowl, combine the chopped dried fruits with brandy or rum, if using. Let them soak for at least 30 minutes to plump up.
3. Prepare Dry Ingredients: In a medium bowl, whisk together the all-purpose flour, baking powder, baking soda, and salt. Set aside.
4. Cream Butter and Sugar: In a large mixing bowl, cream together the softened butter and brown sugar until light and fluffy.
5. Add Egg and Vanilla: Beat in the egg and vanilla extract until well combined.
6. Combine Wet and Dry Ingredients: Gradually add the dry ingredients to the wet ingredients, mixing until just combined.
7. Fold in Fruits and Nuts: Drain any excess liquid from the soaked dried fruits, then fold them into the cookie dough along with the chopped nuts.
8. Scoop Dough: Drop tablespoon-sized portions of dough onto the prepared baking sheets, spacing them about 2 inches apart.
9. Bake: Bake the cookies in the preheated oven for 10-12 minutes, or until lightly golden brown around the edges.
10. Cool: Remove the baking sheets from the oven and let the cookies cool on them for a few minutes before transferring them to wire racks to cool completely.
11. Serve: Once cooled, serve your homemade fruitcake cookies as a delightful holiday treat!

These fruitcake cookies capture the flavors of traditional fruitcake in a more bite-sized and portable form. Enjoy them with a cup of tea or coffee during the holiday season!

Black and White Cookies

Ingredients:

- 2 1/2 cups all-purpose flour
- 1 teaspoon baking powder
- 1/2 teaspoon salt
- 1 cup unsalted butter, softened
- 1 1/2 cups granulated sugar
- 2 large eggs
- 1 teaspoon vanilla extract
- 1/2 cup milk

For the Icing:

- 2 cups confectioners' sugar
- 2 tablespoons unsweetened cocoa powder
- 2-3 tablespoons milk
- 1 teaspoon vanilla extract

Instructions:

1. Preheat Oven: Preheat your oven to 350°F (175°C). Line baking sheets with parchment paper or silicone baking mats.
2. Prepare Dry Ingredients: In a medium bowl, whisk together the all-purpose flour, baking powder, and salt. Set aside.
3. Cream Butter and Sugar: In a large mixing bowl, cream together the softened butter and granulated sugar until light and fluffy.
4. Add Eggs and Vanilla: Beat in the eggs, one at a time, followed by the vanilla extract, until well combined.
5. Alternate Flour and Milk: Gradually add the dry ingredients to the wet ingredients, alternating with the milk, beginning and ending with the dry ingredients. Mix until just combined.
6. Scoop Dough: Drop tablespoon-sized portions of dough onto the prepared baking sheets, spacing them about 2 inches apart.
7. Bake: Bake the cookies in the preheated oven for 10-12 minutes, or until the edges are set and the tops are slightly golden brown. Let them cool on the baking sheets for a few minutes before transferring them to wire racks to cool completely.

8. Prepare Icing: In a medium bowl, whisk together the confectioners' sugar, unsweetened cocoa powder, milk, and vanilla extract until smooth. Adjust the consistency with additional milk, if needed.
9. Ice Cookies: Once the cookies are completely cooled, spread half of each cookie with the chocolate icing and the other half with the vanilla icing. You can use a spoon or offset spatula to spread the icing evenly.
10. Let Set: Allow the icing to set at room temperature for about 30 minutes, or until firm.
11. Serve: Once the icing is set, serve your homemade black and white cookies as a delicious treat!

These classic New York-style black and white cookies are sure to be a hit with their tender texture and delicious combination of vanilla and chocolate icing. Enjoy them with a glass of milk or a cup of coffee for a delightful snack or dessert.